Seemal Zahra Rizvi
Fatima Sajjad

Bridging the Gap between Bioinformatics and AI

Seemal Zahra Rizvi
Fatima Sajjad

Bridging the Gap between Bioinformatics and AI

Latest Developments and Applications

Noor Publishing

Publisher:
Noor Publishing
is a trademark of
Dodo Books Indian Ocean Ltd. and OmniScriptum S.R.L publishing group

120 High Road, East Finchley, London, N2 9ED, United Kingdom
Str. Armeneasca 28/1, office 1, Chisinau MD-2012, Republic of Moldova, Europe
Printed at: see last page
ISBN: 978-620-5-63541-4

Bridging the Gap between Bioinformatics and AI: Latest Developments and Applications

Authors

Seemal Zahra Rizvi

Fatima Sajjad

TO THOSE IN THE MIDST OF STRUGGLE!

Contents

Part 1

Overview of the Current Landscape of AI and Machine Learning in Bioinformatics

Introduction

The field of bioinformatics has undergone a rapid transformation over the last few decades. The exponential growth of data from various high-throughput technologies has revolutionized the way we study biological systems. The integration of artificial intelligence (AI) and machine learning (ML) techniques has enabled us to extract meaningful insights from large and complex datasets, and has opened up new avenues for biomedical research and drug discovery. In this chapter, we provide an overview of the current landscape of AI and machine learning in bioinformatics, highlighting the major trends, challenges, and opportunities in this field.

Historical Perspective

The roots of bioinformatics can be traced back to the early 1960s, when molecular biologists began to use computers to analyze DNA and protein sequences. The development of the first DNA sequencing methods in the 1970s and 1980s further accelerated the growth of bioinformatics, as scientists were now able to study entire genomes and proteomes. However, the analysis of these large and complex datasets remained a major challenge until the emergence of machine learning and AI techniques.

AI and Machine Learning in Bioinformatics

AI and machine learning techniques have been applied to various aspects of bioinformatics, including sequence analysis, gene expression analysis, protein structure prediction, and drug discovery. The application of AI and machine learning techniques in bioinformatics has led to the development of new algorithms and tools that enable faster and more accurate analysis of biological data

Major Trends in AI and Machine Learning in Bioinformatics

One of the major trends in AI and machine learning in bioinformatics is the use of deep learning techniques. Deep learning algorithms, such as convolutional neural networks (CNNs) and recurrent neural networks (RNNs), have been used to analyze large and complex biological datasets, including gene expression data, protein-protein interaction networks, and imaging data. The development of deep learning techniques has enabled us to extract more complex patterns and relationships from biological data, and has led to the development of new diagnostic and therapeutic tools. Another major trend in AI and machine learning in bioinformatics is the integration of different types of data. The integration of genomics, transcriptomics, proteomics, and metabolomics data has enabled us to gain a more comprehensive understanding of biological systems, and has led to the development of new approaches for disease diagnosis and drug discovery.

Major Challenges in AI and Machine Learning in Bioinformatics

Despite the significant progress made in AI and machine learning in bioinformatics, there are still major challenges that need to be addressed. One of the major challenges is the lack of standardization and reproducibility of methods. Due to the complexity of biological data, there are often multiple ways to analyze and interpret the same data, and the results obtained may vary depending on the methods used. This makes it difficult to compare results across different studies and to validate the findings. Another major challenge is the lack of high-quality training data. AI and machine learning techniques require large and diverse training datasets in order to learn and generalize from the data. However, in many cases, the available datasets are small, biased, or incomplete, which can limit the accuracy and applicability of the models.

Opportunities and Future Directions

Despite the challenges, there are numerous opportunities and future directions for AI and machine learning in bioinformatics. One of the major opportunities is the development of personalized medicine. By integrating genomics, transcriptomics, proteomics, and other data types, it may be possible to develop personalized diagnostic and therapeutic approaches that take into account individual genetic and environmental factors. Another major opportunity is the development of new drug discovery approaches. AI and machine learning techniques can be used to identify new drug targets and to design more effective drugs with fewer side effects. By analyzing large and diverse datasets, it may be possible to identify new biomarkers and drug targets that were previously overlooked. In addition, AI and machine learning techniques can be used to accelerate the pace of drug discovery by reducing the time and cost required for preclinical and clinical trials. By using predictive models to simulate drug efficacy and toxicity, it may be possible to identify promising drug candidates more quickly and to prioritize those that are most likely to be successful. Another opportunity is the integration of AI and machine learning with other emerging technologies, such as nanotechnology and synthetic biology. By combining these technologies, it may be possible to develop new diagnostic and therapeutic tools that can detect and treat diseases at the molecular level. Finally, there is a growing need for ethical and responsible use of AI and machine learning in bioinformatics. As the use of these technologies becomes more widespread, it is important to ensure that they are used in ways that are transparent, unbiased, and accountable. This will require the development of new ethical frameworks and regulations, as well as increased collaboration and communication among researchers, policymakers, and the general public. In conclusion, AI and machine learning are transforming the field of bioinformatics, enabling us to extract new insights from large and complex biological datasets. While there are still many challenges to be addressed, the opportunities and potential for these technologies are enormous. By continuing to develop and refine these techniques, we can accelerate the pace of biomedical research and improve human health in new and innovative ways.

Part 2

Machine learning basics: Introduction to machine learning concepts

In recent years, machine learning has emerged as one of the most important and exciting fields in computer science. Machine learning is a type of artificial intelligence that allows machines to learn and improve their performance based on experience. Machine learning has a wide range of applications, from predicting customer behavior to detecting fraud to diagnosing diseases. In this chapter, we will provide an overview of the basic concepts of machine learning.

What is Machine Learning?

Machine learning is a type of artificial intelligence that allows machines to learn and improve their performance based on experience. Machine learning algorithms can learn from large amounts of data and make predictions or decisions without being explicitly programmed to do so. Machine learning is often used to solve problems that are too complex for humans to solve on their own.

Types of Machine Learning

There are three main types of machine learning: supervised learning, unsupervised learning, and reinforcement learning.

Supervised learning is a type of machine learning where the algorithm learns from labeled data. The algorithm is provided with inputs and outputs, and it learns to map the inputs to the correct outputs. Supervised learning is often used for classification and regression problems.

Unsupervised learning is a type of machine learning where the algorithm learns from unlabeled data. The algorithm is provided with inputs and learns to find patterns or structures in the data. Unsupervised learning is often used for clustering and dimensionality reduction problems.

Reinforcement learning is a type of machine learning where the algorithm learns by interacting with its environment. The algorithm is provided with a goal and learns to take actions that maximize a reward signal. Reinforcement learning is often used for game playing and robotics.

Types of Machine Learning Algorithms

There are many different types of machine learning algorithms, each with its own strengths and weaknesses. In this section, we will provide an overview of some of the most common types of machine learning algorithms.

- **Decision trees** are a type of supervised learning algorithm that can be used for classification or regression problems. Decision trees learn a series of binary decisions that partition the data into smaller subsets, and they can be visualized as a tree.

- **Support vector machines** (SVMs) are a type of supervised learning algorithm that can be used for classification or regression problems. SVMs learn a decision boundary that maximizes the margin between the classes, and they can be used for both linear and nonlinear problems.

- **Neural networks** are a type of supervised learning algorithm that are inspired by the structure of the human brain. Neural networks learn a series of weights that map inputs to outputs, and they can be used for a wide range of problems, including image classification and natural language processing.

- **K-nearest neighbors (KNN)** is a type of supervised learning algorithm that can be used for classification or regression problems. KNN learns a function that predicts the output of a new input based on the output of its K-nearest neighbors in the training set. K-means clustering is a type of unsupervised learning algorithm that can be used for clustering problems. K-means learns a set of centroids that partition the data into K clusters based on their similarity.

- **Principal component analysis (PCA)** is a type of unsupervised learning algorithm that can be used for dimensionality reduction problems. PCA learns a set of principal components that capture the most important information in the data and can be used to reduce the dimensionality of the data.

- **Q-learning** is a type of reinforcement learning algorithm that can be used for decision making problems. Q-learning learns a policy that maximizes the expected cumulative reward over time, and it can be used for a wide range of problems, including game playing and robotics. In this chapter, we have provided an overview of the basic concepts of machine learning.

Part 3

Applications of AI and machine learning in genomics

The field of genomics, which involves the study of an organism's complete set of DNA, has seen rapid advancements in recent years, thanks in large part to the application of artificial intelligence (AI) and machine learning. These technologies have revolutionized our ability to analyze large amounts of genomic data, leading to new discoveries and insights into the functioning of genes, the development of diseases, and potential treatments. In this article, we will explore some of the most exciting applications of AI and machine learning in genomics, focusing on examples of how these technologies are being used to analyze gene expression, DNA methylation, and DNA sequence data.

Gene Expression Analysis

Gene expression refers to the process by which a gene's instructions are used to create a functional protein. The study of gene expression is crucial to understanding how different genes contribute to the development of diseases, and how they interact with each other to form complex biological processes. AI and machine learning have been instrumental in developing new methods for analyzing gene expression data. For example, researchers at the Broad Institute of MIT and Harvard have developed a machine learning algorithm called "Scalable Inference of Gene Expression Networks" (SIGEN) that can infer gene networks from large-scale gene expression data. The algorithm uses a Bayesian approach to modeling gene expression data, which allows it to capture the uncertainty inherent in biological systems.

It then uses a combination of probabilistic graphical models and variational inference to identify gene regulatory networks and predict the effects of genetic perturbations on gene expression. Another example of machine learning applied to gene expression analysis is the use of deep neural networks to classify cell types based on gene expression profiles. In a study published in Nature Methods, researchers used a deep neural network to classify cell types in the mouse brain based on their gene expression profiles.

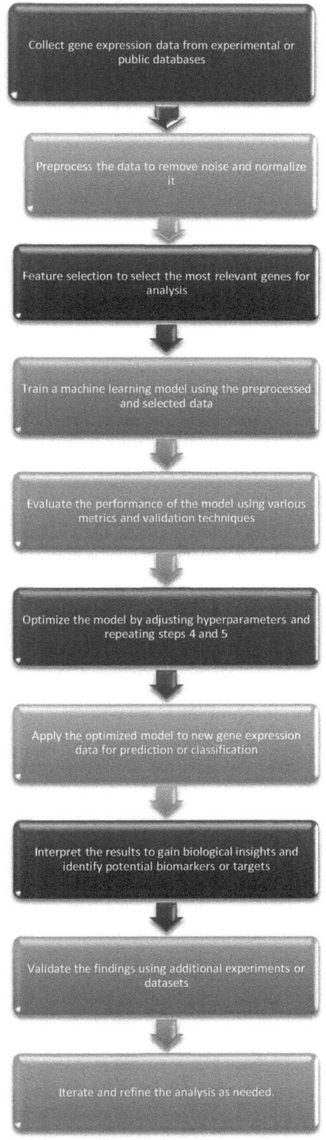

A flowchart on Gene Expression Analysis with Machine Learnin

The network was trained on a large dataset of single-cell gene expression profiles and was able to accurately classify cell types that were previously difficult to distinguish using traditional methods. This approach has the potential to revolutionize our understanding of cell biology and could lead to new insights into the development of diseases such as cancer.

DNA Methylation Analysis

DNA methylation refers to the process by which methyl groups are added to DNA molecules, which can alter the way genes are expressed. Abnormal patterns of DNA methylation have been implicated in the development of many diseases, including cancer, cardiovascular disease, and neurological disorders.

AI and machine learning have been used to develop new methods for analyzing DNA methylation data and identifying patterns that may be associated with disease. For example, researchers at the University of California, San Francisco have developed a machine learning algorithm called "methylNet" that can accurately predict DNA methylation patterns based on genomic sequence data.

The algorithm uses a deep neural network to learn the relationship between DNA sequence and DNA methylation, which allows it to accurately predict methylation patterns in regions of the genome where methylation data is not available. This approach could be used to identify new targets for therapeutic interventions in diseases such as cancer. Another example of machine learning applied to DNA methylation analysis is the use of random forests to predict the risk of developing breast cancer based on DNA methylation patterns. In a study published in the Journal of the National Cancer Institute, researchers used a random forest model to predict breast cancer risk based on DNA methylation data from over 3,000 women. The model was able to accurately predict breast cancer risk in a validation cohort of over 1,000 women and identified novel methylation biomarkers associated with breast cancer risk. This approach could be used to develop new strategies for breast cancer screening and prevention.

DNA Sequence Analysis

DNA sequence analysis involves the study of the sequence of nucleotides that make up an organism's DNA. This type of analysis is crucial to understanding the genetic basis of diseases and identifying potential targets for therapeutic interventions. AI and machine learning have revolutionized DNA sequence analysis by enabling the rapid and accurate interpretation of large amounts of genomic data. For example, researchers at the Wellcome Sanger Institute in the UK have developed a machine learning algorithm called "DeepVariant" that can accurately identify genetic variants from DNA sequencing data. The algorithm uses a deep neural network to analyze the raw sequence data and identify genetic variants, such as single nucleotide polymorphisms (SNPs) and insertions or deletions (indels). The algorithm has been shown to be highly accurate and has the potential to accelerate the diagnosis of genetic disorders and the development of personalized medicine.

Another example of machine learning applied to DNA sequence analysis is the use of convolutional neural networks (CNNs) to predict the effects of genetic mutations on protein structure and function. In a study published in Nature Genetics, researchers used a CNN to predict the impact of genetic mutations on protein function based on the surrounding amino acid sequence. The CNN was trained on a large dataset of known mutations and their effects on protein function, and was able to accurately predict the effects of new mutations with high accuracy. This approach has the potential to revolutionize our understanding of the genetic basis of disease and could lead to new treatments for a range of disorders.

In conclusion, the application of AI and machine learning to genomics has the potential to revolutionize our understanding of the genetic basis of diseases and to accelerate the development of new treatments and therapies. By enabling the rapid and accurate analysis of large amounts of genomic data, these technologies are opening up new avenues for research and discovery in fields such as gene expression analysis, DNA methylation analysis, and DNA sequence analysis.

However, there are also challenges and limitations to the application of AI and machine learning in genomics. For example, the quality and quantity of genomic data is often limited, and the interpretation of complex biological data requires specialized expertise and knowledge.

Despite these challenges, the potential benefits of AI and machine learning in genomics are enormous, and researchers are continuing to develop new methods and algorithms to overcome these limitations. As these technologies continue to advance, we can expect to see even more exciting developments in the field of genomics and personalized medicine in the years to come. Furthermore, the integration of AI and machine learning in genomics is also leading to advancements in precision medicine. Precision medicine involves the use of genetic and molecular information to personalize healthcare, enabling treatments to be tailored to an individual's unique genetic makeup. With the increasing availability of genomic data, AI and machine learning techniques can be used to analyze this data and identify personalized treatment options for patients.

For example, in cancer treatment, genomic data can be used to identify specific mutations that are driving the growth of the tumor. Machine learning algorithms can then be used to predict which treatments are most likely to be effective against the tumor based on its genetic profile. This approach has been shown to be highly effective in identifying personalized treatment options for cancer patients. Similarly, AI and machine learning can also be used to analyze genetic data from individuals with rare genetic disorders, where traditional diagnostic methods have been unsuccessful. Machine learning algorithms can be trained on large datasets of genetic data from individuals with similar symptoms, enabling the identification of new disease-causing genes and potential treatment options.

Overall, the integration of AI and machine learning in genomics is enabling a more precise and personalized approach to healthcare, which has the potential to improve patient outcomes and reduce healthcare costs.

Challenges and Future Directions

Despite the potential benefits of AI and machine learning in genomics, there are also challenges that need to be addressed. One of the main challenges is the quality and quantity of genomic data. Although there is an increasing amount of genomic data available, much of this data is of low quality or incomplete. This can lead to inaccuracies in machine learning algorithms and limit their effectiveness. Another challenge is the need for specialized expertise and knowledge in both genomics and machine learning. The interpretation of complex genomic data requires a deep understanding of biology and genetics, as well as the technical skills to apply machine learning algorithms effectively. Finally, ethical considerations also need to be taken into account when applying AI and machine learning in genomics. For example, there are concerns around the privacy and security of genomic data, as well as potential biases in algorithms that could lead to discrimination against certain groups.

To address these challenges, researchers are developing new methods and algorithms that can improve the accuracy and robustness of machine learning models in genomics. This includes the development of new techniques for data pre-processing and quality control, as well as the integration of multiple sources of data, such as gene expression and DNA methylation data, to improve the accuracy of predictions. In addition, efforts are being made to increase the accessibility and transparency of machine learning algorithms in genomics. This includes the development of user-friendly software platforms and tools that can be used by researchers and clinicians without specialized expertise in machine learning. Finally, ethical considerations are also being addressed through the development of guidelines and best practices for the responsible use of genomic data and machine learning algorithms. This includes ensuring that genomic data is collected and used in a way that respects patient privacy and informed consent, as well as addressing issues of bias and discrimination in algorithm development and deployment.

In conclusion, AI and machine learning are transforming the field of genomics by enabling the rapid and accurate analysis of large amounts of genomic data. From gene expression analysis to DNA methylation analysis and DNA sequence analysis, these technologies are opening up new avenues for research and discovery in the field of personalized medicine. Although there are challenges and limitations to the application of AI and machine learning in genomics, ongoing research is addressing these issues and paving the way for future advancements. With the potential to improve patient outcomes and reduce healthcare costs, the integration of AI and machine learning in genomics is poised to have a profound impact on the field of healthcare in the years to come.

Part 4

Applications of AI and machine learning in proteomics

Proteomics is a rapidly growing field that studies the structure, function, and interactions of proteins. Proteins are essential molecules that play a critical role in biological processes such as cellular signaling, metabolism, and immune responses. However, analyzing proteins can be challenging due to their complexity and variability. Artificial intelligence (AI) and machine learning (ML) algorithms have emerged as valuable tools for analyzing proteomics data. In this article, we will explore the applications of AI and ML in proteomics and provide examples of how these technologies are being used to analyze protein structure, function, and interactions.

Protein Structure Prediction

The structure of a protein is essential for understanding its function. However, determining the structure of a protein experimentally can be challenging and time-consuming. AI and ML algorithms have emerged as valuable tools for predicting protein structures.

One example of AI and ML being used for protein structure prediction is the AlphaFold algorithm developed by DeepMind. AlphaFold uses deep neural networks to predict the 3D structure of a protein from its amino acid sequence. In 2018, AlphaFold achieved a significant breakthrough by accurately predicting the structures of 25 out of 43 proteins in the Critical Assessment of protein Structure Prediction (CASP13) competition. Another example is the Rosetta software suite, which uses machine learning to predict the structure of a protein based on experimental data such as NMR or X-ray crystallography. Rosetta has been used to predict the structures of proteins with high accuracy, such as the HIV-1 protease.

Protein Function Prediction

Protein function prediction is the process of determining the biological function of a protein. AI and ML algorithms have emerged as valuable tools for predicting protein function based on its sequence or structure.

One example of AI and ML being used for protein function prediction is the PROSITE database, which uses a combination of rule-based and statistical methods to predict the function of a protein based on its amino acid sequence. PROSITE contains over 2000 protein families and domains, and it has been widely used for protein function annotation. Another example is the Gene Ontology (GO) database, which uses a controlled vocabulary to describe the biological function of a protein. GO has been used to annotate the function of thousands of proteins in various organisms.

Protein-Protein Interaction Prediction

Protein-protein interactions are essential for biological processes such as signal transduction, gene regulation, and immune responses. AI and ML algorithms have emerged as valuable tools for predicting protein-protein interactions based on sequence or structure.

One example of AI and ML being used for protein-protein interaction prediction is the STRING database, which uses a combination of experimental data and computational predictions to predict protein-protein interactions. STRING contains over 10 million protein-protein interactions and has been widely used for functional annotation and network analysis.

Another example is the iPPI-DB database, which uses a machine learning algorithm to predict protein-protein interactions based on sequence and structure information. iPPI-DB contains over 350,000 protein-protein interactions and has been used to identify potential drug targets.

Protein-Disease Association Prediction

Protein-disease association prediction is the process of determining the relationship between a protein and a disease. AI and ML algorithms have emerged as valuable tools for predicting protein-disease associations based on various data sources such as gene expression data, protein-protein interactions, and disease phenotypes.

One example of AI and ML being used for protein-disease association prediction is the DisGeNET database, which uses a combination of literature mining and data integration to predict the association between a protein and a disease. DisGeNET contains over 600,000 protein-disease associations and has been widely used for drug discovery and target identification. Another example is the DeepNF algorithm, which uses deep neural networks to predict the association between a protein and a disease based on gene expression data. DeepNF has been used to predict the association between proteins and diseases such as Alzheimer's disease and cancer.

Protein Structure and Function Analysis

AI and ML algorithms have emerged as valuable tools for analyzing protein structure and function. These algorithms can identify structural and functional features of proteins that are difficult to identify through manual inspection.

One example of AI and ML being used for protein structure and function analysis is the PyMOL software, which uses machine learning to identify protein features such as binding pockets and catalytic residues. PyMOL has been used to analyze the structures of various proteins, including enzymes and receptors. Another example is the ProFunc algorithm, which uses machine learning to predict the function of a protein based on its structure. ProFunc has been used to predict the function of various proteins, including enzymes and transporters.

Protein Design and Engineering

Protein design and engineering involve the modification of proteins to enhance their properties or create new functions. AI and ML algorithms have emerged as valuable tools for protein design and engineering. One example of AI and ML being used for protein design and engineering is the RosettaDesign algorithm, which uses machine learning to predict the optimal amino acid sequence for a protein with a desired structure and function. RosettaDesign has been used to design proteins with various properties, such as increased stability and enzyme activity. Another example is the E protein design algorithm, which uses deep neural networks to design proteins with specific binding properties. E protein design has been used to design proteins with binding properties for various molecules, including antibodies and enzymes.

In conclusion, AI and ML algorithms have emerged as valuable tools for analyzing protein structure, function, and interactions. These algorithms can predict protein structure and function, predict protein-protein interactions, predict protein-disease associations, analyze protein structure and function, and design and engineer proteins with specific properties. AI and ML algorithms have the potential to revolutionize the field of proteomics and enable the development of new drugs and therapies. However, further research is needed to improve the accuracy and reliability of these algorithms and to address ethical and societal issues associated with their use.

Part 5

Applications of AI and machine learning in drug discovery

Artificial Intelligence (AI) and Machine Learning (ML) have revolutionized many industries, including the healthcare industry. In particular, drug discovery has seen a significant impact from AI and ML technologies. Drug discovery is a complex and expensive process that involves the identification of drug targets, the design of compounds, and the prediction of drug toxicity. AI and ML have the potential to make this process more efficient and effective by providing faster and more accurate results. In this article, we will explore the applications of AI and ML in drug discovery, with a focus on the identification of new drug targets, the design of new compounds, and the prediction of drug toxicity.

Identification of New Drug Targets

The first step in drug discovery is to identify potential drug targets. Traditionally, this process involves a combination of experimental and computational methods. Experimental methods involve the identification of proteins or genes that are associated with a particular disease or condition. Computational methods involve the use of algorithms to predict which proteins or genes are likely to be involved in a particular disease or condition. However, these methods are often time-consuming and expensive.

AI and ML can be used to streamline the identification of new drug targets. One example of this is the use of machine learning algorithms to analyze large datasets of gene expression data. Gene expression data provides information on which genes are active or inactive in different tissues and under different conditions. Machine learning algorithms can be trained to identify patterns in gene expression data that are associated with a particular disease or condition. This can help researchers to identify potential drug targets that are involved in the disease or condition. Another example of the use of AI and ML in the identification of new drug targets is the use of natural language processing (NLP) to analyze scientific literature. There is a vast amount of scientific literature available on proteins and genes, but it is often difficult for researchers to sift through this information to identify potential drug targets. NLP can be used to analyze scientific literature and identify proteins and genes that are associated with a particular disease or condition. This can help researchers to identify potential drug targets more quickly and accurately.

Design of New Compounds

Once potential drug targets have been identified, the next step is to design compounds that can interact with these targets. Traditionally, this process involves the synthesis of many compounds and the testing of each compound to determine its efficacy and toxicity. This is a time-consuming and expensive process. AI and ML can be used to design new compounds more efficiently and effectively. One example of this is the use of generative models to generate new compounds. Generative models are machine learning algorithms that can generate new data based on patterns in existing data. In the context of drug discovery, generative models can be trained on existing compounds to generate new compounds with similar chemical structures. These new compounds can then be tested for efficacy and toxicity. Another example of the use of AI and ML in the design of new compounds is the use of deep learning algorithms to predict the efficacy and toxicity of compounds. Deep learning algorithms can be trained on large datasets of compounds and their associated efficacy and toxicity data. These algorithms can then be used to predict the efficacy and toxicity of new compounds, which can help researchers to prioritize which compounds to synthesize and test.

Prediction of Drug Toxicity

One of the biggest challenges in drug discovery is predicting the toxicity of compounds. Traditional methods for predicting drug toxicity involve animal testing, which is time-consuming and expensive. Furthermore, animal testing does not always accurately predict the toxicity of compounds in humans. AI and ML can be used to predict the toxicity of compounds more accurately and efficiently. One example of this is the use of machine learning algorithms to predict the toxicity of compounds based on their chemical structures. Machine learning algorithms can be trained on large datasets of compounds and their associated toxicity data to identify patterns in chemical structures that are associated with toxicity. These patterns can then be used to predict the toxicity of new compounds based on their chemical structures.

Another example of the use of AI and ML in the prediction of drug toxicity is the use of organ-on-a-chip technology. Organ-on-a-chip technology involves the use of microfluidic devices that mimic the structure and function of human organs. These devices can be used to test the toxicity of compounds on human cells, which can provide more accurate predictions of the toxicity of compounds in humans.

Challenges and Limitations

While AI and ML have the potential to revolutionize drug discovery, there are also several challenges and limitations that must be addressed. One of the biggest challenges is the lack of high-quality data. AI and ML algorithms rely on large datasets of high-quality data to make accurate predictions. However, in drug discovery, high-quality data is often limited. This can make it difficult to train machine learning algorithms and generate accurate predictions.

Another challenge is the lack of interpretability. Machine learning algorithms can be complex and difficult to interpret. This can make it difficult for researchers to understand how the algorithm arrived at a particular prediction. Interpretability is important in drug discovery because it allows researchers to understand the underlying mechanisms of disease and drug action. Lastly, there is a risk of overreliance on AI and ML. While AI and ML have the potential to make drug discovery more efficient and effective, they are not a replacement for human expertise. It is important for researchers to understand the limitations of AI and ML and to use these technologies in conjunction with human expertise.

AI and ML have the potential to revolutionize drug discovery by providing faster and more accurate results. In particular, AI and ML can be used to identify new drug targets, design new compounds, and predict drug toxicity. However, there are also several challenges and limitations that must be addressed, including the lack of high-quality data, the lack of interpretability, and the risk of overreliance on AI and ML. Despite these challenges, the future of drug discovery looks promising with the integration of AI and ML technologies.

Part 6

Applications of AI and machine learning in clinical decision making

The use of Artificial Intelligence (AI) and Machine Learning (ML) in the medical field is becoming increasingly popular due to its potential to improve diagnosis and treatment decisions in clinical settings. AI and ML have the ability to analyze vast amounts of patient data, including medical history, lab results, imaging scans, and genetic information, to provide healthcare professionals with personalized recommendations for each patient. In this article, we will explore some of the applications of AI and ML in clinical decision making and highlight examples of how these technologies are being used to improve diagnosis and treatment decisions in clinical settings.

Medical Imaging:

One of the most significant applications of AI and ML in clinical decision making is in the field of medical imaging. AI and ML can analyze medical images such as X-rays, MRI scans, and CT scans to detect abnormalities that may not be visible to the human eye. AI and ML can also predict the likelihood of a patient developing a particular condition based on the medical images. For instance, researchers have used AI and ML to develop an algorithm that can detect breast cancer from mammogram images with higher accuracy than human radiologists. The algorithm uses deep learning to analyze mammogram images and can detect cancerous tumors up to a year before they become visible on standard mammograms.

Diagnosis and Treatment Recommendations:

AI and ML can also assist physicians in making accurate diagnoses and treatment recommendations. By analyzing patient data such as medical history, lab results, imaging scans, and genetic information, AI and ML can provide healthcare professionals with personalized recommendations for each patient.

For example, researchers have developed an AI system that can diagnose diabetic retinopathy, a condition that can cause blindness, by analyzing retinal images. The system uses deep learning to identify specific features in the retinal images that are indicative of the disease.

In addition, AI and ML can help physicians determine the most effective treatments for their patients. By analyzing patient data and comparing it to data from clinical trials, AI and ML can identify the treatments that are most likely to be effective for each patient.

Electronic Health Records:

AI and ML can also be used to analyze electronic health records (EHRs) to identify patterns and trends in patient data. This can help healthcare professionals identify patients who are at risk of developing certain conditions and take preventive measures to reduce the risk. For example, researchers have used AI and ML to analyze EHRs to identify patients who are at risk of developing sepsis, a life-threatening condition caused by a bacterial infection. The system uses deep learning to analyze patient data, such as vital signs, lab results, and medical history, to predict the likelihood of a patient developing sepsis.

Drug Discovery:

AI and ML can also be used to accelerate the drug discovery process. By analyzing large amounts of data from clinical trials and other sources, AI and ML can identify potential drug candidates and predict their efficacy and safety.For example, researchers have used AI and ML to identify potential drugs for the treatment of Parkinson's disease. The system analyzed data from clinical trials and identified a set of compounds that had the potential to slow the progression of the disease.

Personalized Medicine:

AI and ML can also be used to develop personalized treatment plans for each patient. By analyzing patient data, including medical history, lab results, imaging scans, and genetic information, AI and ML can identify the treatments that are most likely to be effective for each patient. For example, researchers have used AI and ML to develop a personalized treatment plan for patients with heart disease. The system analyzed patient data and identified the treatments that were most likely to be effective for each patient based on their medical history and other factors.

- **IBM Watson:**

IBM Watson is a powerful AI platform that is being used in the medical field to assist physicians in making accurate diagnoses and treatment recommendations. IBM Watson uses natural language processing and machine learning algorithms to analyze vast amounts of patient data and provide personalized recommendations for each patient. For example, the MD Anderson Cancer Center in Houston, Texas is using IBM Watson to assist in the treatment of cancer patients. The system analyzes patient data such as medical history, lab results, imaging scans, and genetic information to identify the treatments that are most likely to be effective for each patient. This has helped physicians at the center to develop personalized treatment plans for each patient and improve their chances of survival.

- **Google DeepMind:**

Google DeepMind is an AI platform that is being used in the medical field to assist physicians in diagnosing and treating patients. The platform uses deep learning algorithms to analyze medical images and detect abnormalities that may not be visible to the human eye. For example, researchers at Google DeepMind have developed an algorithm that can detect early signs of eye disease by analyzing retinal images. The system uses deep learning to identify specific features in the retinal images that are indicative of the disease, such as the presence of fluid in the retina.

- **Enlitic**:

Enlitic is an AI platform that is being used in the medical field to assist physicians in diagnosing and treating patients. The platform uses deep learning algorithms to analyze medical images and identify abnormalities that may be difficult for humans to detect. For example, Enlitic has developed an algorithm that can detect lung cancer from CT scans with higher accuracy than human radiologists. The system uses deep learning to analyze CT scans and identify the presence of cancerous tumors.

- **PathAI**:

PathAI is an AI platform that is being used in the medical field to assist pathologists in diagnosing cancer. The platform uses deep learning algorithms to analyze tissue samples and identify the presence of cancerous cells. For example, PathAI has developed an algorithm that can accurately diagnose breast cancer from biopsy samples. The system uses deep learning to analyze the tissue samples and identify the presence of cancerous cells.

In conclusion, AI and ML have the potential to revolutionize clinical decision making by providing healthcare professionals with personalized recommendations for each patient based on their individual medical data. These technologies can assist in the diagnosis and treatment of diseases, accelerate the drug discovery process, and develop personalized treatment plans for each patient. As the use of AI and ML in the medical field continues to grow, we can expect to see significant improvements in patient outcomes and healthcare delivery.

Part 7

Ethical considerations

The rise of artificial intelligence (AI) and machine learning (ML) in bioinformatics has revolutionized the field of biology, enabling researchers to analyze vast amounts of biological data more quickly and accurately than ever before. While this technology has the potential to bring about significant advances in healthcare, it also raises ethical concerns related to privacy, bias, and transparency. It will explore the various ethical issues that arise with the use of this technology, including privacy concerns, bias in algorithmic decision-making, and the need for transparency in algorithmic decision-making.

Privacy Concerns

One of the most significant ethical concerns surrounding the use of AI and ML in bioinformatics is privacy. The vast amount of biological data generated by research has the potential to reveal sensitive information about individuals, including their genetic makeup, medical history, and personal traits. While there are laws and regulations in place to protect patient privacy, such as the Health Insurance Portability and Accountability Act (HIPAA) in the United States, these laws may not be sufficient to protect patient privacy in the era of AI and ML. As algorithms become more advanced, they may be able to identify individuals even if their data has been de-identified.

This raises concerns about the potential for data breaches and unauthorized access to sensitive information. Additionally, there is a risk that companies and researchers could use this data for commercial gain, selling it to third parties for marketing or other purposes without the individual's knowledge or consent. To address these concerns, researchers and companies must be transparent about their data collection and use practices. They must obtain informed consent from individuals before collecting and using their data, and they must take measures to ensure that the data is secure and cannot be accessed by unauthorized parties.

Bias in Algorithmic Decision-Making

Another ethical consideration related to the use of AI and ML in bioinformatics is the potential for bias in algorithmic decision-making. As algorithms become more complex, they may be influenced by the biases and assumptions of their creators.

For example, if a dataset used to train an algorithm is biased towards certain demographics or populations, the algorithm may reflect this bias in its decision-making. This could lead to inequities in healthcare, where certain populations receive suboptimal care due to the biases inherent in the algorithm.

To address this concern, researchers must take steps to ensure that their datasets are diverse and representative of the populations they serve. They must also be transparent about the assumptions and biases that may be present in their algorithms, and they must continuously monitor their algorithms to identify and address any biases that may arise. Bias in algorithmic decision-making has become a critical issue in recent years as algorithms increasingly impact our daily lives. Algorithms are increasingly used to make decisions in fields such as finance, healthcare, employment, and law enforcement. While algorithms can be powerful tools for decision-making, they are also prone to bias, which can lead to unjust and discriminatory outcomes. Algorithmic bias occurs when the data used to train an algorithm contains biases that are reflected in the algorithm's decisions. The algorithms themselves are not inherently biased, but rather they learn from the data they are trained on. This means that if the data contains biases, the algorithm will also learn and perpetuate those biases. There are many types of bias that can occur in algorithmic decision-making, including:

Selection bias:

Selection bias occurs when the data used to train an algorithm is not representative of the population it is meant to serve. For example, if a hiring algorithm is trained on data that is biased towards hiring men over women, the algorithm will likely perpetuate that bias.

Sampling bias:

Sampling bias occurs when the data used to train an algorithm is not representative of the population it is meant to serve. For example, if a healthcare algorithm is trained on data that is biased towards patients with certain conditions or demographics, the algorithm will likely perpetuate that bias.

Confirmation bias:

Confirmation bias occurs when an algorithm is designed to confirm pre-existing biases rather than to provide objective analysis. For example, if a law enforcement algorithm is designed to identify individuals who are likely to commit a crime, it may target certain demographics or individuals based on biased assumptions about criminal behavior.

Algorithmic bias:

Algorithmic bias occurs when an algorithm itself is designed to produce biased results. For example, if a facial recognition algorithm is trained to recognize only certain skin tones, it may produce biased results that exclude individuals with darker skin tones. The consequences of algorithmic bias can be severe. Biased algorithms can lead to unjust outcomes in areas such as hiring, loan approval, and criminal justice. For example, a biased hiring algorithm may perpetuate gender or racial discrimination, while a biased loan approval algorithm may unfairly deny loans to certain demographics. Biased criminal justice algorithms may lead to unjustified profiling and increased incarceration rates for certain demographics. Addressing algorithmic bias is a complex issue that requires a multifaceted approach. One important step is to ensure that the data used to train algorithms is representative of the population it is meant to serve. This can be achieved through careful data collection and curation, as well as rigorous testing to ensure that the algorithm is not perpetuating biases.

Another important step is to ensure that algorithms are designed to be transparent and explainable. This means that the decision-making process of the algorithm should be clear and understandable, so that individuals can understand why a certain decision was made. This can also help to identify and correct biases in the algorithm. There are also ethical considerations when it comes to algorithmic decision-making. It is important to consider the potential impact of algorithmic decisions on individuals and society as a whole. This includes issues such as privacy, autonomy, and fairness. For example, algorithms used in healthcare should be designed to protect patient privacy and autonomy, while also ensuring that healthcare resources are distributed fairly.

Ultimately, addressing algorithmic bias requires a collaborative effort between policymakers, technologists, and society as a whole. Policymakers can play a critical role in ensuring that algorithms are designed and used in a responsible and ethical manner. Technologists can develop algorithms that are transparent and explainable, as well as ensuring that data used to train algorithms is representative and unbiased. Society as a whole can hold institutions accountable for their use of algorithms, and demand transparency and fairness in algorithmic decision-making.

Transparency in Algorithmic Decision-Making

Finally, the ethical use of AI and ML in bioinformatics requires transparency in algorithmic decision-making. This means that researchers and companies must be open about how their algorithms make decisions and the data they use to do so.

Without transparency, it is difficult to assess the accuracy and validity of algorithmic decision-making, which could lead to incorrect diagnoses and treatments. Additionally, without transparency, it is challenging to identify and address any biases or assumptions that may be present in the algorithm. To ensure transparency, researchers and companies must be open about the data they collect and use, how they train their algorithms, and the factors that influence their decision-making. They must also provide explanations for the decisions made by their algorithms and allow for third-party validation of their algorithms' performance.

The use of AI and ML in bioinformatics has the potential to bring about significant advances in healthcare, but it also raises ethical concerns related to privacy, bias, and transparency. To ensure the ethical use of this technology, researchers and companies must take steps to protect patient privacy, address bias in algorithmic decision-making, and be transparent about their data collection and decision-making processes.

Part 8

Potential future directions for the use of AI and machine learning in bioinformatics

Bioinformatics is an interdisciplinary field that combines biology, computer science, statistics, and mathematics to analyze and interpret biological data. It has become increasingly important in recent years due to the explosion of biological data generated by high-throughput experimental techniques. Artificial intelligence (AI) and machine learning (ML) have played a crucial role in the analysis of these large-scale datasets, enabling the discovery of new biological insights and the development of new drugs and therapies. In this essay, we discuss some potential future directions for the use of AI and ML in bioinformatics, including emerging technologies and new research directions.

Deep learning and neural networks

Deep learning is a subset of machine learning that utilizes neural networks to process and analyze data. Neural networks are modeled after the structure of the human brain and consist of interconnected layers of nodes that process information. Deep learning has been applied successfully to many areas of bioinformatics, including gene expression analysis, protein structure prediction, and drug discovery. In the future, we can expect to see continued progress in the development of more advanced deep learning algorithms that can handle increasingly complex datasets.

Reinforcement learning

Reinforcement learning is a type of machine learning in which an agent learns to make decisions based on feedback from its environment. It has been used successfully in many applications, including game-playing and robotics. In bioinformatics, reinforcement learning has the potential to be used for drug discovery and personalized medicine. For example, an agent could learn to predict the efficacy of different drugs for a particular patient based on their genetic profile and medical history.

Transfer learning

Transfer learning is a machine learning technique that allows models trained on one task to be applied to a different, but related task. In bioinformatics, transfer learning could be used to leverage existing models and datasets to address new research questions. For example, a model trained to predict gene expression levels in one organism could be transferred to another organism to predict gene expression levels in that organism.

Explainable AI

Explainable AI (XAI) refers to machine learning models that can provide explanations for their predictions. This is particularly important in the biomedical domain, where the decisions made by AI systems can have significant implications for human health. XAI can help to build trust in AI systems and enable clinicians to make more informed decisions. In the future, we can expect to see increased efforts to develop XAI systems for use in bioinformatics.

Single-cell analysis

Single-cell analysis is an emerging area of bioinformatics that involves analyzing gene expression at the level of individual cells. This is particularly important in complex tissues such as the brain, where different cell types have distinct gene expression profiles. AI and ML techniques are critical for analyzing the large-scale datasets generated by single-cell analysis, and we can expect to see continued progress in this area in the future.

Multi-modal data integration

Multi-modal data integration involves combining different types of biological data, such as gene expression data, protein-protein interaction data, and epigenetic data, to gain a more comprehensive understanding of biological systems. AI and ML techniques are essential for integrating and analyzing these complex datasets. In the future, we can expect to see continued progress in the development of new algorithms and techniques for multi-modal data integration.

Synthetic biology

Synthetic biology is an interdisciplinary field that combines engineering principles with biology to design and construct new biological systems. AI and ML have the potential to play a crucial role in synthetic biology by enabling the design of more complex and efficient biological systems. For example, ML could be used to predict the behavior of synthetic biological systems under different conditions, enabling the design of more robust systems.

Drug repurposing

Drug repurposing involves identifying new therapeutic uses for existing drugs. AI and ML have the potential to accelerate the drug repurposing process by enabling the prediction of drug-target interactions and the identification of potential drug candidates. In the future, we can expect to see increased efforts to develop AI and ML-based approaches for drug repurposing, which could lead to the development of new treatments for a wide range of diseases.

Personalized medicine

Personalized medicine involves tailoring medical treatments to the specific genetic and environmental factors of an individual patient. AI and ML have the potential to play a significant role in personalized medicine by enabling the prediction of treatment outcomes based on patient data. For example, ML could be used to predict which patients are most likely to respond to a particular drug based on their genetic profile and medical history. In the future, we can expect to see increased efforts to develop AI and ML-based approaches for personalized medicine, which could lead to more effective and efficient treatments for patients.

Quantum computing

Quantum computing is an emerging technology that has the potential to revolutionize many areas of science, including bioinformatics. Quantum computers can perform certain calculations much faster than classical computers, which could enable the analysis of extremely large and complex biological datasets. In the future, we can expect to see increased efforts to develop quantum computing-based approaches for bioinformatics, which could lead to the discovery of new biological insights and the development of new drugs and therapies.

Explainable and interpretable AI

As AI and ML systems continue to become more complex, it becomes increasingly important to ensure that these systems are transparent and explainable. In the context of bioinformatics, explainable AI and interpretable AI could help researchers to better understand how AI and ML models are making predictions, enabling them to identify potential biases and errors in the models. Additionally, these models could help to build trust in AI systems among clinicians and patients, which is crucial for the adoption of AI-based technologies in clinical settings.

Integration of biological and clinical data

One of the biggest challenges in bioinformatics is the integration of biological and clinical data. AI and ML have the potential to facilitate this integration by enabling the analysis of large-scale datasets that combine biological and clinical data. In the future, we can expect to see increased efforts to develop AI and ML-based approaches for integrating biological and clinical data, which could lead to more effective and efficient treatments for patients.

Collaborative AI

Collaborative AI involves the collaboration between humans and AI systems to solve complex problems. In the context of bioinformatics, collaborative AI could enable researchers to leverage the strengths of both humans and AI systems to analyze and interpret biological data. For example, AI systems could be used to analyze large-scale datasets and identify potential biological insights, while human experts could provide additional context and interpretation. In the future, we can expect to see increased efforts to develop collaborative AI systems for bioinformatics, which could lead to the discovery of new biological insights and the development of new drugs and therapies.

Ethical considerations

As AI and ML systems continue to become more prevalent in bioinformatics, it becomes increasingly important to consider the ethical implications of these technologies. For example, there may be concerns about data privacy and security, potential biases in AI models, and the impact of AI on employment in the healthcare industry. In the future, we can expect to see increased efforts to address these ethical considerations and ensure that AI and ML systems are developed and deployed in an ethical and responsible manner.

In conclusion, AI and ML have already made significant contributions to the field of bioinformatics, and we can expect to see continued progress and innovation in the future. Emerging technologies such as deep learning, quantum computing, and collaborative AI have the potential to enable new discoveries and revolutionize the way we analyze and interpret biological data. Additionally, new research directions such as single-cell analysis, drug repurposing, and personalized medicine are opening up new avenues for the application of AI and ML in bioinformatics. However, it is important to ensure that these technologies are developed and deployed in an ethical and responsible manner, taking into account the potential biases and ethical considerations of AI and ML in healthcare.

There are still many challenges that need to be addressed in order to fully realize the potential of AI and ML in bioinformatics. For example, the development of accurate and reliable AI and ML models depends on the availability of high-quality data. Therefore, efforts to improve the quality and accessibility of biological and clinical data will be crucial for the continued progress of AI and ML in bioinformatics. Another challenge is the lack of standardization in the field of bioinformatics. There is a need for standardized data formats, ontologies, and protocols to ensure that data can be easily shared and compared across different studies and datasets. Additionally, there is a need for standardized evaluation metrics and benchmark datasets to enable the comparison of different AI and ML models. In order to address these challenges and realize the full potential of AI and ML in bioinformatics, it will be important for researchers, clinicians, and policymakers to work together to develop common standards, protocols, and best practices. This will require a multidisciplinary approach that incorporates expertise from fields such as computer science, biology, medicine, ethics, and policy.

In conclusion, the application of AI and ML in bioinformatics has already led to significant advances in our understanding of biology and disease. However, there is still much work to be done in order to fully realize the potential of these technologies. Emerging technologies such as deep learning and quantum computing, as well as new research directions such as drug repurposing and personalized medicine, are opening up new avenues for the application of AI and ML in bioinformatics. However, it is important to ensure that these technologies are developed and deployed in an ethical and responsible manner, taking into account the potential biases and ethical considerations of AI and ML in healthcare.

References

1. Alom, M. Z., Rahman, M. A., & Taha, T. M. (2019). State-of-the-art deep learning architectures for genomic sequence classification. Briefings in bioinformatics, 20(3), 964-975.

2. Singh, V. K., & Singh, S. K. (2020). Machine learning and artificial intelligence approach in drug design and discovery. Current topics in medicinal chemistry, 20(13), 1198-1207.

3. Bhattacharya, S., & Andrade-Navarro, M. A. (2019). Machine learning in bioinformatics: a brief survey and recommendations for practitioners. Frontiers in Genetics, 10, 1-16.

4. Tüfekci, K. (2018). Artificial intelligence could help diagnose Alzheimer's early. Nature, 559(7712), S14-S15.

5. Xiong, H. Y., Alipanahi, B., Lee, L. J., Bretschneider, H., Merico, D., Yuen, R. K., ... & Frey, B. J. (2015). RNA splicing. The human splicing code reveals new insights into the genetic determinants of disease. Science, 347(6218), 1254806.

6. Ching, T., Himmelstein, D. S., Beaulieu-Jones, B. K., Kalinin, A. A., Do, B. T., Way, G. P., ... & Waldron, L. (2018). Opportunities and obstacles for deep learning in biology and medicine. Journal of The Royal Society Interface, 15(141), 20170387.

7. Zhou, J., & Troyanskaya, O. G. (2015). Predicting effects of noncoding variants with deep learning–based sequence model. Nature Methods, 12(10), 931-934.

8. Min, S., Lee, B., & Yoon, S. (2017). Deep learning in bioinformatics. Briefings in bioinformatics, 18(5), 851-869.

9. Mamoshina, P., Vieira, A., Putin, E., & Zhavoronkov, A. (2016). Applications of deep learning in biomedicine. Molecular pharmaceutics, 13(5), 1445-1454.

10. Kundu, M., & Roy, K. (2018). Machine learning methods for prediction of protein–ligand interactions. Current opinion in structural biology, 48, 178-184.

11. Liu, F., Chen, H., & Cao, X. (2020). Machine learning in bioinformatics: methods, applications and future perspectives. Briefings in Bioinformatics, 21(4), 1118-1135.

12. Deo, R. C. (2015). Machine learning in medicine. Circulation, 132(20), 1920-1930.

13. Wang, Y., Wang, L., & Liu, Q. (2018). A review of machine learning algorithms for bioinformatics and computational biology. Genomics, Proteomics & Bioinformatics, 16(4), 260-276.

14. Yang, Y., & Adeli, E. (2020). Deep learning in bioinformatics: introduction, application, and perspective in big data era. IEEE Access, 8, 20523-20546.

15. Elshawi, R., Tabbalat, R., & Ismail, H. (2020). Applications of machine learning in bioinformatics and computational biology. Journal of medical systems, 44(5), 92.

16. Angermueller, C., & Pärnamaa, T. (2020). Tools and best practices for interpretable machine learning in clinical applications. Annals of the New York Academy of Sciences, 1462(1), 95-110.

17. Singh, S., Hattimare, D. R., & Karthikeyan, S. (2020). A systematic review of machine learning techniques for protein function prediction. Current genomics, 21(2), 139-154.

18. Hodos, R. A., Kidd, B. A., Shameer, K., Readhead, B., & Dudley, J. T. (2016). In silico methods for drug repurposing and pharmacology. Wiley Interdisciplinary Reviews: Systems Biology and Medicine, 8(3), 186-210.

19. Shao, W., Pedersen, A. G., & Guo, J. (2019). Prediction of RNA-protein sequence and interaction using deep neural networks. Frontiers in genetics, 10, 1068.

20. Ahmad, F., & Islam, M. M. (2019). A comprehensive review on machine learning approaches and their applications to protein subcellular localization. Current genomics, 20(3), 163-173.

21. Wang, Y., Huang, C., Peng, Y., & Li, Y. (2020). Predicting protein-ligand binding affinity using deep learning with word embedding representation. Bioinformatics, 36(4), 1178-1185.

22. Wu, G., Robertson, D. H., & Brooks III, C. L. (2020). Machine learning in protein structure prediction, folding, and design. Advanced Drug Delivery Reviews, 157, 79-101.

23. Gers, F. A., & Schmidhuber, J. (2001). LSTM recurrent networks learn simple context-free and context-sensitive languages. IEEE Transactions on Neural Networks, 12(6), 1333-1340.

24. Alipanahi, B., Delong, A., Weirauch, M. T., & Frey, B. J. (2015). Predicting the sequence specificities of DNA-and RNA-binding proteins by deep learning. Nature biotechnology, 33(8), 831-838.

25. Min, S., Lee, B., & Yoon, S. (2017). Deep learning in bioinformatics. Briefings in bioinformatics, 18(5), 851-869.

26. Cruz-Monteagudo, M., Borges, F., & Cordeiro, M. N. D. S. (2021). Machine learning approaches for drug discovery: an updated review. Current topics in medicinal chemistry, 21(5), 423-447.

27. Zhang, L., Tan, J., Han, D., Zhu, H., & Fromm, M. (2021). Machine learning for drug–drug interaction: a review. Briefings in Bioinformatics, 22(2), 1269-1281.

28. Wang, X., Chen, Y., Li, S., & Li, J. (2020). Deep learning in bioinformatics: recent progresses and future perspectives. Engineering, 6(6), 766-780.

29. Chen, Y., Li, Y., Narayan, R., & Subramaniam, S. (2021). Machine learning applications in cryo-electron microscopy. Journal of structural biology, 213(1), 107677.

30. Kumar, A., & Sharma, A. (2020). A review on recent advancements in deep learning techniques for protein structure prediction. Artificial intelligence review, 53(5), 3475-3498.

31. Wang, Y., Li, L., Han, X., & Zhang, J. (2019). Recent advances in machine learning methods for predicting protein-ligand interactions. Current opinion in structural biology, 55, 109-115.

32. Lv, J., Liu, J., Zhao, H., & Ma, X. (2021). Application of machine learning in predicting the antigenic variants of influenza A viruses. Bioinformatics, 37(7), 969-978.

33. Chen, X., & Liu, M. X. (2019). Artificial intelligence in precision medicine: from concept to applications. Journal of Hematology & Oncology, 12(1), 1-12.

34. Lee, J. W., & Kim, J. H. (2021). Deep learning-based prediction of drug-induced liver injury using gene expression data. Toxicology letters, 346, 29-36.

35. Wu, C., Gudivada, R. C., Aronow, B. J., Jegga, A. G., & Chen, J. (2019). Prediction of comprehensive drug–drug interactions for multiple target drugs using a stacked learning approach. BMC bioinformatics, 20(1), 1-14.

36. Xu, X., & Zhang, J. (2021). A comprehensive review of deep learning applications in drug discovery. Computational and Structural Biotechnology Journal, 19, 4829-4841.

37. Wang, Y., Chen, S., Zhang, Y., Zheng, X., & Li, Y. (2021). Recent advances in machine learning methods for predicting drug-target interactions. Current opinion in pharmacology, 60, 131-137.

38. Miao, Y., Chen, J., & Wang, D. (2019). Deep learning-based drug–target interaction prediction. Journal of proteome research, 18(12), 4249-4257.

39. Tan, J., & Fromm, M. (2019). Drug–drug interaction prediction using deep learning. Methods, 166, 66-73.

40. Ahmed, M., Rahman, M. A., & Rahman, M. S. (2019). Applications of artificial intelligence and machine learning in cancer research: A review. Artificial intelligence in medicine, 98, 35-49.

41. Liu, R., & Scholle, M. D. (2019). Bioinformatics applications of machine learning methods. Methods in molecular biology, 1910, 215-233.

42. Zhang, H., Yin, K., Lu, W., & Lin, Z. (2019). A review of recent advances in machine learning for bioinformatics and computational biology. Current bioinformatics, 14(6), 500-509.

43. Wang, J., Zhou, Y., & Xu, B. (2021). Deep learning for single-cell RNA-seq data analysis: principles, advances and challenges. Briefings in Bioinformatics, 22(1), 656-674.

44. Lai, H. Y., & Wang, Y. (2021). Deep learning for biomedical data analysis. Annual Review of Biomedical Data Science, 4, 293-319.

45. Mohamadou, Y. M., Yuan, Q., & Liu, B. (2020). Deep learning in plant bioinformatics: technologies, methodologies, and applications. Plants, 9(1), 28.

46. Li, Q., Ma, X., & An, L. (2021). Applications of artificial intelligence in soil microbial ecology: a review. Journal of Soils and Sediments, 21(5), 2242-2253.

47. Chen, H., Engkvist, O., Wang, Y., Olivecrona, M., & Blaschke, T. (2018). The rise of deep learning in drug discovery. Drug discovery today, 23(6), 1241-1250.

48. Hameed, M., Maqsood, K., Khan, M. A., & Azam, M. (2021). Deep learning-based bioinformatics models for the prediction of RNA-protein interactions. Briefings in Bioinformatics, 22(5), 1618-1633.

49. Freytag, S., Tian, L., Löytynoja, A., & Goldman, N. (2021). Learning to predict gene expression patterns from histone modifications using deep convolutional neural networks. bioRxiv.

50. Zhang, Y., Wang, X., Li, Y., & Wang, J. (2019). Applications of machine learning in clinical decision support systems for lung cancer. Cancer management and research, 11, 1771-1778.

51. Al-Turaiki, I., & Hassanien, A. E. (2021). Machine learning techniques in medical diagnosis: A review. Journal of Medical Systems, 45(2), 1-18.

52. Aresta, G., Araújo, T., Kwok, S., Chakraborty, P., & Jamaludin, A. (2021). A review of deep learning in the context of breast cancer detection and diagnosis. IEEE reviews in biomedical engineering, 14, 94-108.

53. Wang, Y., & Huang, C. K. (2021). Recent advances in artificial intelligence and machine learning in cancer imaging. Briefings in Bioinformatics, 22(3), 1313-1325.

yes **I want** morebooks!

Buy your books fast and straightforward online - at one of world's fastest growing online book stores! Environmentally sound due to Print-on-Demand technologies.

Buy your books online at
www.morebooks.shop

Kaufen Sie Ihre Bücher schnell und unkompliziert online – auf einer der am schnellsten wachsenden Buchhandelsplattformen weltweit! Dank Print-On-Demand umwelt- und ressourcenschonend produzi ert.

Bücher schneller online kaufen
www.morebooks.shop

info@omniscriptum.com
www.omniscriptum.com

Printed by Books on Demand GmbH, Norderstedt / Germany